June 1997

Dear Miss Shanks,

Thank you so much for teaching Rachel with such enthusiasm and effort during her Primary 2 year.

May God bless you in the rest of your teaching career and "outside" life.

With very best wishes,

Sheela & Trevor
Ramsey.

FAMOUS HYMNS

AND THEIR STORIES

Compiled by Christopher Idle

SANDY
LANE
BOOKS

Text copyright © 1987 Christopher Idle
This edition copyright © 1987 Lion Publishing

Published by
Sandy Lane Books
Sandy Lane West, Oxford, England
ISBN 0 7459 4001 3
Albatross Books Pty Ltd
PO Box 320, Sutherland, NSW 2232, Australia
ISBN 0 7324 1339 7

First edition 1987
This edition 1995
10 9 8 7 6 5 4 3 2 1 0

All the hymns and most of the extracts printed here first appeared in
The Lion Book of Favourite Hymns and later in *Hymns of Praise* and *Songs of Faith*.

Acknowledgments
'Tell out my soul' is reproduced by kind permission of Timothy Dudley-Smith
Scripture quotations from the Holy Bible, New International Version,
copyright New York International Bible Society, 1978

Photographs by Sonia Halliday Photographs as follows:
F.H.C. Birch pages 9, 21, 46, 51, 61, 65; Sister Daniel pages 22, 27, 28, 31,
32, 35, 38, 53, 59, 86, 91; Sonia Halliday pages 11, 12, 19, 36, 42, 44, 62, 66, 71,
75, 79, 85, 93 and endpapers; Laura Lushington pages 15, 69, 77, 80, 89;
Barrie Searle page 48; Jane Taylor page 56; Else Trickett pages 16, 24,
41, 54, 73; Barbara Warley page 83

A catalogue record for this title is available
from the British Library.

Printed and bound in Singapore

CONTENTS

PRAISE, MY SOUL,
THE KING OF HEAVEN

A tiny and remote country parish in
Southern Ireland did not seem the ideal place for the brilliant
young graduate to start his ministry — six feet tall with dark,
curly hair, a classical scholar with great gifts as a speaker. But
here in County Wexford, as a brash new curate, Henry Francis
Lyte had an encounter which turned his ideas inside out.

A neighbouring clergyman was terminally ill.
He confessed to Lyte that he had begun to re-examine his life
as he read and studied the New Testament. He urged his
younger friend to do what he had at last done: to stop relying
on religious duties and good deeds for his peace with God, but
trust completely in the mercy of Christ and his saving power.

This meeting immediately checked Lyte's
contempt for the Methodists and 'enthusiasts' in the area. It
gave him for the first time a truly personal faith. And it
inspired him to write hymns such as this famous version of
Psalm 103.

Praise, my soul, the King of heaven;
　To his feet thy tribute bring.
Ransomed, healed, restored,
　forgiven,
　Who like thee his praise should
　sing?
Praise him! Praise him!
Praise the everlasting King.

Praise him for his grace and favour
　To our fathers in distress;
Praise him still the same for ever,
　Slow to chide, and swift to bless.
Praise him! Praise him!
Glorious in his faithfulness.

Father-like, he tends and spares us;
　Well our feeble frame he knows;
In his hands he gently bears us,
　Rescues us from all our foes.
Praise him! Praise him!
Widely as his mercy flows.

Angels in the height, adore him;
　Ye behold him face to face;
Sun and moon, bow down before
　him;
　Dwellers all in time and space.
Praise him! Praise him!
Praise with us the God of grace.

HENRY FRANCIS LYTE (1793-1847)

LET ALL THE WORLD
IN EVERY CORNER SING

As a young man, George Herbert did not give much thought to God. But when he was thirty-six, he left the political rat-race of the court of King James I to become the rector of a country parish near Salisbury.

One of Herbert's great joys was music. Twice a week he would walk into Salisbury to play and sing with his friends at the cathedral.

One day he stopped on the way to help a man whose horse had collapsed in the mud under its load. The group of friends in Salisbury were surprised when Herbert, usually so smart and clean, arrived 'so soiled and discomposed'. One said he had 'disparaged himself by so dirty an employment'.

Herbert replied that the thought of what he had done would be music to him at midnight — and that the omission of it would have made discord in his conscience. 'I am bound to practise what I pray for . . . and I praise God for this occasion. Come, let's tune our instruments!'

Let all the world in every corner sing,
    My God and King!
The heavens are not too high,
His praise may thither fly;
The earth is not too low,
His praises there may grow.
Let all the world in every corner sing,
    My God and King!

Let all the world in every corner sing,
    My God and King!
The church with psalms must shout,
No door can keep them out;
But above all, the heart
Must bear the longest part.
Let all the world in every corner sing,
    My God and King!

GEORGE HERBERT (1593-1632)

O FOR A THOUSAND TONGUES TO SING

Charles Wesley was never quite sure of his own birthday. It was, after all, just before Christmas; he was his mother's eighteenth child, born some weeks premature, so small and frail that he seemed more dead than alive. For two months he neither cried nor opened his eyes.

But he was quite sure of the date of what he called his second birth' — 21 May 1738. On that day he responded to the love and grace of God. He wrote this hymn a year later, 'For the anniversary day of one's conversion'.

O for a thousand tongues to sing
  My great Redeemer's praise,
The glories of my God and King,
  The triumphs of his grace!

Jesus! the name that charms our
    fears,
  That bids our sorrows cease;
'Tis music in the sinner's ears,
  'Tis life, and health, and peace.

He breaks the power of cancelled
    sin,
  He sets the prisoner free;
His blood can make the foulest
    clean,
  His blood availed for me.

He speaks, and, listening to his
    voice,
  New life the dead receive,
The mournful, broken hearts rejoice,
  The humble poor believe.

Hear him, ye deaf; his praise, ye
    dumb,
  Your loosened tongues employ;
Ye blind, behold your Saviour come,
  And leap, ye lame, for joy.

My gracious Master and my God,
  Assist me to proclaim,
To spread through all the earth
    abroad
  The honours of thy name.

CHARLES WESLEY (1707–88)

TELL OUT, MY SOUL,
THE GREATNESS OF THE LORD

The seventeenth century was the great age of Bible translation. Parts of the eighteenth and nineteenth were boom periods for new hymns. The second half of the twentieth century has seen a flood of exciting new versions of the Bible in English as well as an upsurge of contemporary hymn-writing.

When Timothy Dudley-Smith was sent a review copy of the 1961 *New English Bible*, he was very struck by the beginning of Luke's Gospel. In this version, the *Magnificat*, or 'Song of Mary', begins with the words 'Tell out, my soul, the greatness of the Lord'. They inspired him to write this paraphrase, which is now one of the most popular of modern hymns. It is the only hymn in our book by a living author, but it stands as a reminder that the tradition of writing and singing new Christian songs is thriving today.

Tell out, my soul, the greatness of the Lord!
Unnumbered blessings, give my spirit voice;
Tender to me the promise of his word;
In God my Saviour shall my heart rejoice.

Tell out, my soul, the greatness of his name!
Make known his might, the deeds his arm has done;
His mercy sure, from age to age the same;
His holy name — the Lord, the Mighty One.

Tell out, my soul, the greatness of his might!
Powers and dominions lay their glory by.
Proud hearts and stubborn wills are put to flight,
The hungry fed, the humble lifted high.

Tell out, my soul, the glories of his word!
Firm is his promise, and his mercy sure.
Tell out, my soul, the greatness of the Lord
To children's children and for evermore!

TIMOTHY DUDLEY-SMITH (b. 1926)

ALL PEOPLE
THAT ON EARTH DO DWELL

The Swiss city of Geneva conjures up different images for different people. Some may remember holidays among lake and mountain scenery; others think of the United Nations and international diplomacy. It has also come to stand for the religious tradition of the Puritans, and the historic 'Geneva Bible'.

Even in the sixteenth century, Geneva was a great 'united nations' — of refugees fleeing from religious persecution. Among them was Scotsman William Kethe, who shared in translating the Bible and wrote this enduring hymn, based on Psalm 100. Its famous tune, written by a Frenchman, is known as the 'Old Hundredth'.

All people that on earth do dwell,
Sing to the Lord with cheerful
voice;
Him serve with fear, his praise
forth tell,
Come ye before him, and rejoice.

The Lord, ye know, is God indeed,
Without our aid he did us make;
We are his folk, he doth us feed,
And for his sheep he doth us
take.

For why? the Lord our God is
good:
His mercy is for ever sure;
His truth at all times firmly stood,
And shall from age to age
endure.

O enter then his gates with praise,
Approach with joy his courts
unto;
Praise, laud, and bless his name
always,
For it is seemly so to do.

To Father, Son, and Holy Ghost,
The God whom heaven and
earth adore,
From men and from the angel-host
Be praise and glory evermore.

WILLIAM KETHE (d. 1594)

GLORIOUS THINGS
OF THEE ARE SPOKEN

Today we usually expect a service in church
to start with a hymn. But 200 years ago it was different —
only the psalms could be sung.

John Newton played an important part in the
battle to have hymns accepted in church. While in Liverpool,
he and his wife Mary would often spend an hour on Sunday
evenings praying and singing with friends. In his first parish
as a minister, at Olney in Buckinghamshire, the week-night
meeting where this hymn was first sung soon had to move to
larger premises. And on Sundays, Newton's ministry·
attracted so many to the services that a gallery had to be built
in the church to make room for everybody!

Glorious things of thee are spoken,
   Zion, city of our God;
He whose word cannot be broken
   Formed thee for his own abode.
On the Rock of ages founded,
   What can shake thy sure repose?
With salvation's walls surrounded,
   Thou may'st smile at all thy foes.

See! the streams of living waters,
   Springing from eternal love,
Well supply thy sons and daughters,
   And all fear of want remove.
Who can faint while such a river
   Ever flows their thirst to assuage?
Grace which, like the Lord the giver,
   Never fails from age to age.

Round each habitation hovering,
   See the cloud and fire appear
For a glory and a covering,
   Showing that the Lord is near.
Thus they march, the pillar leading,
   Light by night and shade by day;
Daily on the manna feeding
   Which he gives them when
      they pray.

Saviour, if of Zion's city
   I through grace a member am,
Let the world deride or pity,
   I will glory in thy name.
Fading is the worldling's pleasure,
   All his boasted pomp and show;
Solid joys and lasting treasure
   None but Zion's children know.

NOW
THANK WE ALL OUR GOD

Germany in the seventeenth century was in the throes of the Thirty Years' War. Martin Rinkart was a Lutheran pastor in the walled city of Eilenberg in Saxony. In spite of his frail physique, he stayed there throughout the war, enduring the horrors of famine and plague. He helped refugees from other areas who came to the city. When all the other pastors had either fled or died, he ministered to the sick and dying, and conducted some 4,500 funerals, including that of his own wife. Towards the end of the war, the city was besieged or overrun, once by the Austrians and twice by the Swedes. The Swedish general demanded a vast levy from Eilenberg's already desperate citizens; Martin pleaded with him, but in vain. So he turned to his friends and said, 'Come, my children; we can find no mercy with man — let us take refuge with God.' The general was so moved at seeing pastor and people praying and singing on their knees that the demand was reduced to less than a twentieth of the original sum.

This hymn, which began as a family grace said before meals, was sung as a national thanksgiving at the end of the Thirty Years' War.

Now thank we all our God
  With hearts and hands and voices,
Who wondrous things hath done,
  In whom his world rejoices;
Who from our mother's arms
  Hath blessed us on our way
With countless gifts of love,
  And still is ours today.

O may this bounteous God
  Through all our life be near us,
With ever joyful hearts
  And blessèd peace to cheer us;
And keep us in his grace,
  And guide us when perplexed,
And free us from all ills
  In this world and the next.

All praise and thanks to God
  The Father now be given,
The Son, and Holy Ghost,
  Supreme in highest heaven;
The one eternal God,
  Whom earth and heaven adore
For thus it was, is now,
  And shall be evermore.

MARTIN RINKART (1586-1649)
translated by CATHERINE WINKWORTH (1827-78)

HOLY, HOLY, HOLY

'Dad, when was the first Trinity Sunday?'
Dad could not answer that perfectly serious and innocent
question quite as easily as he could talk about the first
Christmas or the first Easter.

Trinity Sunday is the one festival in the church's year
marking not an event but a fact — the truth about the nature
of God himself. And the words of 'Holy, holy, holy' stand
almost alone among hymns; they simply attempt to describe,
and worship, the three persons of the Godhead. Reginald
Heber wrote them for one Trinity Sunday at his parish church
in Shropshire.

When Heber was only forty, he became Bishop of Calcutta.
But three years of travel and responsibility for the whole of
India broke his health. Many of his stirring missionary hymns
were published after his death.

Holy, Holy, Holy! Lord God
    Almighty!
  Early in the morning our song
    shall rise to thee;
Holy, Holy, Holy! Merciful and
    mighty!
  God in three Persons, blessed
    Trinity!

Holy, Holy, Holy! though the
    darkness hide thee,
  Though the eye of sinful man
    thy glory may not see,
Only thou art holy, there is none
    beside thee
  Perfect in power, in love, and
    purity.

Holy, Holy, Holy! all the saints
    adore thee,
  Casting down their golden
    crowns around the glassy sea;
Cherubim and seraphim falling
    down before thee,
  Which wert, and art, and
    evermore shalt be.

Holy, Holy, Holy! Lord God
    Almighty!
  All thy works shall praise thy
    name, in earth, and sky, and
    sea;
Holy, Holy, Holy! Merciful and
    mighty!
  God in three Persons, blessed
    Trinity!

REGINALD HEBER (1783–1826)

HOW SWEET
THE NAME OF JESUS SOUNDS

Neither John Newton's language nor his talent for verse had always been used for sacred purposes. In his early days on board ship, he taught the rest of the crew a song he had composed; what the lyrics said about the captain, his character, his family and his ship, was unprintable — like most of Newton's general conversation.

Another captain under whom he served was so appalled by Newton's constant blasphemy that when the weather turned stormy, he was convinced that he had a Jonah on board: Newton would have to go!

His conversion to Jesus Christ brought about startling changes for Newton, and this hymn is clear evidence that his mouth had had a spring-clean! He now used the name of Jesus in a new way, and his gift for choice words had been completely redirected.

How sweet the name of Jesus
   sounds
  In a believer's ear!
It soothes his sorrows, heals his
   wounds,
  And drives away his fear.

It makes the wounded spirit whole,
  And calms the troubled breast;
'Tis manna to the hungry soul,
  And to the weary rest.

Dear name! the rock on which I
   build,
  My shield and hiding-place.
My never-failing treasury filled
  With boundless stores of grace.

Jesus! my Shepherd, Husband,
   Friend,
  My Prophet, Priest, and King,
My Lord, my Life, my Way, my
   End,
  Accept the praise I bring.

Weak is the effort of my heart,
  And cold my warmest thought;
But when I see thee as thou art,
  I'll praise thee as I ought.

Till then I would thy love proclaim
  With every fleeting breath;
And may the music of thy name
  Refresh my soul in death.

JOHN NEWTON (1725–1807)

ALL CREATURES
OF OUR GOD AND KING

Francis of Assisi was born into a wealthy
Italian family. His father, a cloth merchant, was furious when
Francis was converted to Jesus Christ and took seriously the
words in the Gospels about giving to the poor.

Turning his back on a life of luxury, Francis travelled
around the countryside with a few followers, preaching God's
love for every living creature. He loved God's world of nature
and saw all created things as objects of love which point to
their Creator. And in the growing cities, he preached the
gospel while living in utter poverty among ordinary people.

In the last year of his short life, ill, in pain and almost
blind, Francis wrote his *Canticle of the Sun*, beginning 'All
creatures of our God and King'. It was an early Italian version
of the church's *Benedicite* — 'O all ye works of the Lord, bless
ye the Lord'.

All creatures of our God and King,
Lift up your voice and with us sing
 Alleluia, Alleluia!
Thou burning sun with golden beam,
Thou silver moon with softer gleam:
O praise him, O praise him,
Alleluia, Alleluia, Alleluia!

Thou flowing water, pure and clear,
Make music for thy Lord to hear,
 Alleluia, Alleluia!
Thou fire so masterful and bright,
That givest man both warmth and
 light:

And all ye men of tender heart,
Forgiving others, take your part,
 O sing ye, Alleluia!
Ye who long pain and sorrow bear,
Praise God and on him cast your care;

Let all things their Creator bless,
And worship him in humbleness;
 O praise him, Alleluia!
Praise, praise the Father, praise the Son,
And praise the Spirit, Three in One;

FRANCIS OF ASSISI (1182–1226)
translated by WILLIAM DRAPER (1855–1933)

ALL THINGS
BRIGHT AND BEAUTIFUL

The chief writer of hymns for children in the nineteenth century was undoubtedly Mrs Cecil Frances Alexander, whose husband became primate of all Ireland. She wanted to help children understand the Christian faith. Of her 400 hymns, several were written to explain the meaning of phrases from the Apostles' Creed. 'All things bright and beautiful' explains in language children can understand the Creed's opening words: 'I believe in God, the Father Almighty, Maker of heaven and earth.'

All things bright and beautiful,
All creatures great and small,
All things wise and wonderful,
The Lord God made them all.

Each little flower that opens,
Each little bird that sings,
He made their glowing colours,
He made their tiny wings.

The purple-headed mountain,
The river running by,
The sunset, and the morning
That brightens up the sky.

The cold wind in the winter,
The pleasant summer sun,
The ripe fruits in the garden,
He made them every one.

The tall trees in the greenwood,
The meadows where we play,
The rushes by the water
We gather every day:

He gave us eyes to see them,
And lips that we might tell
How great is God Almighty
Who has made all things well.

CECIL FRANCES ALEXANDER (1818-95)

LET US,
WITH A GLADSOME MIND

'Either teach or learn, or leave': the motto, painted in Latin on the windows of St Paul's School in London, was hardly needed by John Milton, one of its brightest pupils.

He had 'a delicate, tuneable voice' and had inherited his father's love of music and books. He often sat up well after midnight to study Latin or Greek by candlelight. When he complained of headaches and tired eyes, no one recognized the warning signs; in his early forties he became totally blind.

Milton was fifteen, in his last year at St Paul's in 1623, when he wrote these lines. He put Psalm 136 into English verse, perhaps as a school exercise. This version makes him the youngest contributor to many hymn-books.

Let us, with a gladsome mind,
Praise the Lord, for he is kind:
For his mercies aye endure,
Ever faithful, ever sure.

Let us blaze his name abroad,
For of gods he is the God:

He with all-commanding might
Filled the new-made world with
   light:

Caused the golden-tressèd sun
All day long his course to run:

The hornèd moon to shine by night
'Mongst her spangled sisters bright:

He his chosen race did bless
In the wasteful wilderness:

He hath, with a piteous eye,
Looked upon our misery:

All things living he doth feed;
His full hand supplies their need:

Let us therefore warble forth
His great majesty and worth:

JOHN MILTON (1608–74)

WE PLOUGH THE FIELDS

This hymn was written by a layman. The author of the original German words was in turn a Commissioner of Agriculture and Manufacture, a newspaper editor and a bank auditor. His Christian faith wavered under the influence of the eighteenth-century view that man was his own saviour and master of his own destiny. But after a serious illness he turned again to the Maker of all things, and the heavenly Father who loves and cares for his children.

He wrote this hymn as part of a dramatic sketch; its theme was the festival of harvest thanksgiving at a German farmhouse.

We plough the fields, and scatter
  The good seed on the land,
But it is fed and watered
  By God's almighty hand:
He sends the snow in winter,
  The warmth to swell the grain,
The breezes and the sunshine,
  And soft refreshing rain:
All good gifts around us
  Are sent from heaven above;
Then thank the Lord, O thank the Lord,
  For all his love.

He only is the maker
  Of all things near and far,
He paints the wayside flower,
  He lights the evening star.
The winds and waves obey him,
  By him the birds are fed;
Much more to us, his children,
  He gives our daily bread:

We thank thee, then, O Father,
  For all things bright and good,
The seed-time and the harvest,
  Our life, our health, our food:
Accept the gifts we offer
  For all thy love imparts,
And, what thou most desirest,
  Our humble, thankful hearts.

MATTHIAS CLAUDIUS (1740-1815)
translated by JANE M. CAMPBELL (1817-78)

WHEN I SURVEY
THE WONDROUS CROSS

Five-year-old Isaac Watts was asked by his
father why he had giggled in the middle of their solemn family
prayers. He said that through his fingers he had seen a mouse
running up the bell-rope, and had suddenly thought,

'There was a mouse, for want of stairs,
Ran up a rope to say his prayers'!

But it wasn't until he was about twenty that
he ventured to complain to his father about the grim verse of
the metrical psalms they had to sing at Above Bar Chapel in
Southampton. 'Try then whether you can yourself produce
something better,' was the answer.

The young man who had learned Latin at
four, Greek at nine, French at ten and Hebrew at thirteen, sat
down to write straight away, and never looked back. In all,
he wrote about 750 hymns. Many people regard this as the
greatest of them all.

When I survey the wondrous cross
  On which the Prince of glory died,
My richest gain I count but loss,
  And pour contempt on all my
    pride.

Forbid it, Lord, that I should boast
  Save in the death of Christ my
    God;
All the vain things that charm me
    most,
  I sacrifice them to his blood.

See from his head, his hands, his feet,
  Sorrow and love flow mingled
    down!
Did e'er such love and sorrow meet,
  Or thorns compose so rich a
    crown?

His dying crimson like a robe,
  Spreads o'er his body on the tree;
Then am I dead to all the globe,
  And all the globe is dead to me.

Were the whole realm of nature
    mine,
  That were a present far too small;
Love so amazing, so divine,
  Demands my soul, my life, my all.

ISAAC WATTS (1674-1748)

THERE IS A GREEN HILL

Mrs Alexander was the daughter of a major and the wife of a bishop. She was a tireless visitor, going from cottage to cottage in all weathers, supporting her husband's work in his diocese in Northern Ireland.

This hymn, dating from before her marriage, was written at the bedside of a child who was ill. The profits from *Hymns for Little Children*, where it first appeared in print, went to a school for deaf and dumb children in Londonderry. And Mendelssohn's friend William Horsley, who wrote the famous tune, was organist for eighteen years at a home for orphan girls in London.

The girl for whom the words were written recovered from her illness, and always regarded the hymn as especially hers, even when she grew up. Its greatness lies in the fact that so many other adults have done the same.

There is a green hill far away
  Outside a city wall,
Where the dear Lord was crucified,
  Who died to save us all.

We may not know, we cannot tell,
  What pains he had to bear,
But we believe it was for us
  He hung and suffered there.

He died that we might be forgiven,
  He died to make us good,
That we might go at last to heaven,
  Saved by his precious blood.

There was no other good enough
  To pay the price of sin;
He only could unlock the gate
  Of heaven, and let us in.

O dearly, dearly has he loved,
  And we must love him too,
And trust in his redeeming blood,
  And try his works to do.

CECIL FRANCES ALEXANDER (1818-95)

ROCK OF AGES

It was August 1756. A small group of people was meeting in a wooden barn in a village in Southern Ireland. The speaker, a layman named Morris, could hardly spell his own name, but he could read and understand the apostle Paul's words in Ephesians: 'But now in Christ Jesus ye who sometimes were far off are made nigh by the blood of Christ.' And, as he spoke, sixteen-year-old Augustus Toplady put his trust in Christ for the first time.

Toplady's most famous hymn grew from a single four-line verse appearing in *The Gospel Magazine*. He could be a bitter and obsessive controversialist, but this hymn has outlasted all his volumes of argument.

Rock of ages, cleft for me,
Let me hide myself in thee.
Let the water and the blood
From thy riven side which flowed
Be of sin the double cure,
Cleanse me from its guilt and power.

Not the labours of my hands
Can fulfil thy law's demands;
Could my zeal no respite know,
Could my tears for ever flow,
All for sin could not atone;
Thou must save, and thou alone.

Nothing in my hand I bring;
Simply to thy cross I cling;
Naked, come to thee for dress,
Helpless, look to thee for grace;
Foul, I to the fountain fly:
Wash me, Saviour, or I die!

While I draw this fleeting breath,
When my eyelids close in death;
When I soar through tracts unknown,
See thee on thy judgement throne,
Rock of ages, cleft for me,
Let me hide myself in thee.

AND CAN IT BE

In spite of their differing temperaments, brothers John and Charles Wesley did many things together. At Oxford they formed the 'Holy Club' and earned the name of 'Methodist'; in Georgia they were none-too-successful missionaries; in London in 1738 they each found the experience that brought them peace with God. They also published hymn-books together. Although no one is quite sure which of the brothers wrote this hymn, Charles usually gets the credit.

He was converted to a living, personal faith while staying with a brazier called John Bray, who lived almost under the shadow of St Paul's Cathedral. On the Sunday when his 'chains fell off', Charles read in his *Book of Common Prayer* from Psalm 40: 'He hath put a new song in my mouth: even a thanksgiving unto our God.'

For the man who wrote nearly 7,000 new songs of praise to God, those were prophetic words.

And can it be that I should gain
  An interest in the Saviour's
    blood?
Died he for me, who caused his
    pain?
  For me, who him to death
    pursued?
Amazing love! how can it be
That thou, my God, shouldst die
    for me!

He left his Father's throne above,
  So free, so infinite his grace,
Emptied himself of all but love,
  And bled for Adam's helpless
    race.
'Tis mercy all, immense and free;
For, O my God, it found out me!

Long my imprisoned spirit lay
  Fast bound in sin and nature's
    night;
Thine eye diffused a quickening ray —
  I woke, the dungeon flamed
    with light;
My chains fell off, my heart was free,
I rose, went forth, and followed
    thee.

No condemnation now I dread;
  Jesus, and all in him, is mine!
Alive in him, my living head,
  And clothed in righteousness
    divine,
Bold I approach the eternal throne,
And claim the crown, through
    Christ, my own.

CHARLES WESLEY (1707–88)

JESUS LIVES!

The German Lutheran who wrote this hymn was known for his bad memory — and his generous spirit.

As assistant pastor to his father, he could not remember his own sermons well enough to preach without notes — and reading the sermon was frowned on. So he became a lecturer instead, and as Professor of Philosophy he filled his lecture-room to overflowing.

His kindness overflowed too. He gave away so much that when Prince Henry of Prussia visited him, he found him living in one empty room without food or fire. But, if only with this one Easter hymn, he has made many others rich.

Jesus lives! thy terrors now
Can, O death, no more appal us;
Jesus lives! by this we know
Thou, O grave, canst not
enthral us. Alleluia!

Jesus lives! henceforth is death
But the gate of life immortal;
This shall calm our trembling
breath,
When we pass its gloomy
portal. Alleluia!

Jesus lives! for us he died;
Then, alone, to Jesus living,
Pure in heart may we abide.
Glory to our Saviour giving.
Alleluia!

Jesus lives! our hearts know well
Nought from us his love shall
sever;
Life, nor death, nor powers of hell
Tear us from his keeping ever.
Alleluia!

Jesus lives! to him the throne
Over all the world is given;
May we go where he is gone,
Rest and reign with him in
heaven. Alleluia!

CHRISTIAN GELLERT (1715–69)
translated by FRANCES COX (1812–97)

THE HEAD THAT ONCE
WAS CROWNED WITH THORNS

Thomas Kelly was the son of an Irish judge.
He was ordained but fell foul of his bishop and founded his
own sect, which nearly died with him. But this hymn has.
stood the test of time.

Kelly's practical faith was put to the test during a year of
severe famine. He was loved by the poorest of the people for
his kindness. One man cheered up his anxious wife by saying,
'Hold up, Bridget — there's always Mister Kelly to pull us out
of the mire after we've sunk for the last time!'

The head that once was crowned
    with thorns
  Is crowned with glory now:
A royal diadem adorns
  The mighty Victor's brow.

The highest place that heaven
    affords
  Is his, is his by right,
The King of kings and Lord of
    lords,
  And heaven's eternal Light:

The joy of all who dwell above,
  The joy of all below,
To whom he manifests his love,
  And grants his name to know.

To them the cross, with all its
    shame,
  With all its grace is given:
Their name an everlasting name,
  Their joy the joy of heaven.

They suffer with their Lord below,
  They reign with him above,
Their profit and their joy to know
  The mystery of his love.

The cross he bore is life and health,
  Though shame and death to
    him;
His people's hope, his people's
    wealth,
  Their everlasting theme.

THOMAS KELLY (1769–1855)

AMAZING GRACE

A violent storm at sea was the turning-point in John Newton's life.

Motherless at six and sent to sea on his eleventh birthday, he soon became a teenage rebel. He was press-ganged into the navy and flogged for desertion. Newton became involved with the African slave-trade and came close to starvation while living in extreme poverty in Sierra Leone.

But in March 1748, at the age of twenty-three, he was on board a cargo ship which was fighting for its life against heavy seas and rough weather. Worn out with pumping and almost frozen, he called out for God's mercy at the height of the storm, and was amazed to be saved from almost certain death.

Newton's life had many twists and turns. Eventually he renounced his involvement with slave-trading and, at thirty-nine, became a minister in the church. He persuaded the young William Wilberforce to stay in politics, and joined him in the fight to abolish the slave-trade.

Amazing grace! how sweet the sound
That saved a wretch like me!
I once was lost, but now am found,
Was blind, but now I see.

'Twas grace that taught my heart
   to fear,
  And grace my fears relieved;
How precious did that grace appear
  The hour I first believed!

The Lord has promised good to me,
  His word my hope secures;
He will my shield and portion be
  As long as life endures.

Through many dangers, toils, and
   snares
  I have already come;
'Tis grace that brought me safe thus
   far
  And grace will lead me home.

Yes, when this heart and flesh shall
   fail
  And mortal life shall cease
I shall possess within the veil
  A life of joy and peace.

JOHN NEWTON (1725-1807)

JESUS LOVES ME

In October 1949 Chairman Mao Tse Tung declared the establishment of the People's Republic of China. It quickly became apparent that all western Christians would have to leave the country. Soon mainland China was closed to Christians outside.

The church in China went through a very hard time. The little news that did leak out had to be discreet. And in one message received in 1972, there was a sentence which read, 'The *this I know* people are well.'

To the authorities the words did not make sense. But such is the international language of Christian songs that friends outside the bamboo curtain knew immediately that their fellow-believers were in good heart.

Jesus loves me, this I know,
For the Bible tells me so;
Little ones to him belong,
They are weak, but he is strong.

Jesus loves me! He who died
Heaven's gate to open wide;
He will wash away my sin,
Let his little child come in.

Yes, Jesus loves me;
    yes, Jesus loves me;
Yes, Jesus loves me,
    the Bible tells me so.

ANNA WARNER (1820–1915)

TO GOD BE THE GLORY!

Fanny Crosby, the American singer and musician, was blind from the age of six weeks. She married her music teacher, Alexander Van Alstyne, who was also blind. She once signed an unusual contract with a publisher: to write three songs every week all through the year. In all she wrote many thousands.

Although American evangelists Moody and Sankey used this hymn on their missions, it did not become an immediate favourite. But Billy Graham featured it in his Harringay crusade in 1954 — and soon Londoners were singing it on their way home, in streets and bus queues and underground trains.

Dr Graham took it back to the United States, introduced it next at Nashville, Tennessee, and saw it take its place in the group of top favourites.

To God be the glory! great things he hath done!
So loved he the world that he gave us his Son.
Who yielded his life an atonement for sin,
And opened the life-gate that all may go in.

Praise the Lord! Praise the Lord! Let the earth hear
his voice!
Praise the Lord! Praise the Lord! Let the people rejoice!
O come to the Father through Jesus the Son;
And give him the glory — great things he hath done!

O perfect redemption, the purchase of blood!
To every believer the promise of God;
The vilest offender who truly believes,
That moment from Jesus a pardon receives.

Great things he hath taught us, great things he hath done,
And great our rejoicing through Jesus the Son:
But purer and higher and greater will be
Our wonder, our transport, when Jesus we see!

FANNY CROSBY (1820-1915)

LOVE DIVINE

Court composer Henry Purcell and Poet Laureate John Dryden were a powerful combination in late seventeenth-century England. When they got together to write a patriotic song — part of the opera *King Arthur* — it was an ideal partnership:

'Fairest Isle, all isles excelling,
Seat of pleasures and of loves,
Venus here will choose her dwelling
And forsake her Cyprian groves . . .

But for Charles Wesley, a generation later, this was just not good enough. Venus, Jove and Cupid, he felt, were getting more than enough honours paid to them; so he wrote these new words to be sung to Purcell's tune.

Instead of pagan legends, Wesley's verses are full of the Bible; instead of glorifying the mythical deities of Mount Olympus, he wrote in praise of Jesus.

Love divine, all loves excelling,
Joy of heaven, to earth come down!
Fix in us thy humble dwelling,
All thy faithful mercies crown:
Jesu, thou art all compassion,
Pure, unbounded love thou art:
Visit us with thy salvation,
Enter every trembling heart.

Come, almighty to deliver,
Let us all Thy grace receive;
Suddenly return, and never,
Never more thy temples leave:
Thee we would be always blessing,
Serve thee as thy hosts above,
Pray, and praise thee, without ceasing,
Glory in thy perfect love.

Finish then thy new creation,
Pure and spotless let us be;
Let us see thy great salvation,
Perfectly restored in thee;
Changed from glory into glory,
Till in heaven we take our place,
Till we cast our crowns before thee,
Lost in wonder, love and praise!

CHARLES WESLEY (1707-88)

TAKE MY LIFE

Frances Ridley Havergal was a natural musician and could have been a professional singer. She was not strong physically — she 'hoped the angels would have orders to let her alone a bit when she first got to heaven' — but she worked hard and used her musical and linguistic gifts to the full. This hymn was written on the last night of a five-day visit to a friend's home, where she wanted everyone to commit themselves wholeheartedly to God and experience his blessings.

She lived out the words in her hymns, too. She once wrote to another friend: ' "Take my silver and my gold" now means shipping off all my ornaments — including a jewel cabinet which is really fit for a countess — to the Church Missionary Society . . . I retain only a brooch for daily wear, which is a memorial of my dear parents; also a locket . . . I had no idea I had such a jeweller's shop . . . I don't think I need tell you I never packed a box with such pleasure.'

Take my life, and let it be
Consecrated, Lord, to thee;
Take my moments and my days,
Let them flow in ceaseless praise.

Take my hands, and let them move
At the impulse of thy love.
Take my feet, and let them be
Swift and beautiful for thee.

Take my voice, and let me sing
Always, only, for my King;
Take my lips, and let them be
Filled with messages from thee.

Take my silver and my gold;
Not a mite would I withhold;
Take my intellect, and use
Every power as thou shalt choose.

Take my will, and make it thine:
It shall be no longer mine.
Take my heart; it is thine own:
It shall be thy royal throne.

Take my love; my Lord, I pour
At thy feet its treasure-store.
Take myself, and I will be
Ever, only, all, for thee.

GUIDE ME,
O THOU GREAT JEHOVAH

It was a fiery open-air sermon by Howell Harris, the Welsh evangelist, that gave to young medical student William Williams a new ambition and a new vocation.

And it was open-air preaching that Williams himself took up after an abortive start in the Church of England ministry. For almost half a century he travelled over the mountains, roads and tracks of Wales, averaging some 3,000 miles a year on horseback or on foot. Of the 800 hymns that he wrote in Welsh, this is his greatest. The tune 'Cwm Rhondda' did not appear until the twentieth century, but it is now inseparable from the words. And Welshmen are unrivalled singers of it, not least in the open air.

Guide me, O thou great Jehovah,
  Pilgrim through this barren land;
I am weak, but thou art mighty,
  Hold me with thy powerful
    hand:
  Bread of heaven,
Feed me till I want no more.

Open now the crystal fountain,
  Whence the healing stream doth
    flow;
Let the fire and cloudy pillar
  Lead me all my journey through:
  Strong Deliverer,
Be thou still my strength and
    shield.

When I tread the verge of Jordan,
  Bid my anxious fears subside;
Death of death, and hell's
    destruction,
  Land me safe on Canaan's side:
  Songs of praises
I will ever give to thee.

WILLIAM WILLIAMS (1717-91)
translated by PETER WILLIAMS (1722-96) and others

THE LORD'S MY SHEPHERD

A voyage from Britain to India in 1830 was nearly a disaster. A ship was wrecked in a violent storm off the Cape of Good Hope. No lives were lost, but almost everything else was. Alexander Duff, educational statesman and the first missionary sent to India by the Presbyterian Church of Scotland, lost an entire personal library — all except two books: his Bible and a Scottish Psalm Book were washed ashore. He took that as a parable. From now on he would concentrate on essentials.

In India, his household began each day by singing a psalm. And the words of Psalm 23 came vividly to his mind as he saw a shepherd leading his sheep across a precipitous track in the northern mountains. The man carried a long rod, with a hook at one end to help the sheep, and an iron band at the other for beating off wild animals. The rod and the staff, said Duff, were both needed — for guidance and defence.

This Scottish version of the twenty-third psalm is the consistent favourite among metrical psalms sung today.

The Lord's my shepherd, I'll not want;
　He makes me down to lie
In pastures green; he leadeth me
　The quiet waters by.

My soul he doth restore again,
　And me to walk doth make
Within the paths of righteousness,
　E'en for his own name's sake.

Yea, though I walk in death's dark vale,
　Yet will I fear none ill,
For thou art with me, and thy rod
　And staff me comfort still.

My table thou hast furnishèd
　In presence of my foes;
My head with oil thou dost anoint
　And my cup overflows.

Goodness and mercy all my life
Shall surely follow me;
And in God's house for evermore
My dwelling-place shall be.

SCOTTISH PSALTER (1650)

A SAFE STRONGHOLD
OUR GOD IS STILL

Martin Luther was the leading figure of the Reformation of the church in Germany in the sixteenth century. As an obscure monk studying at a university, he rediscovered for himself that the only way to God was through faith in Jesus Christ.

It was a time when ordinary people were being promised a way out of hell if they would give money to rebuild St Peter's Church in Rome. Luther spoke out against such abuses. He was keen that people should read and understand the Bible for themselves, so he translated the New Testament from Greek into German. He introduced the German language into church services, which had previously been conducted in Latin. Luther also led the way in congregational hymn-singing, setting new words to the popular tunes of the day.

A safe stronghold our God is still,
　A trusty shield and weapon.
He'll help us clear from all the ill
　That hath us now o'ertaken.
　　The ancient prince of hell
　　Hath risen with purpose fell;
　　Strong mail of craft and power
　　He weareth in this hour;
On earth is not his fellow.

With force of arms we nothing can;
　Full soon were we down-ridden.
But for us fights the proper Man
　Whom God himself hath bidden.
　　Ask ye, Who is this same?
　　Christ Jesus is his name,
　　The Lord Sabaoth's Son;
　　He, and no other one,
Shall conquer in the battle.

And were this world all devils o'er,
　And watching to devour us.
We lay it not to heart so sore;
　Not they can overpower us.
　　And let the prince of ill
　　Look grim as e'er he will,
　　He harms us not a whit;
　　For why? his doom is writ —
A word shall quickly slay him.

God's word, for all their craft and force,
　One moment will not linger,
But, spite of hell, shall have its course;
　'Tis written by his finger.
　　And though they take our life,
　　Goods, honour, children, wife,
　　Yet is their profit small;
　　These things shall vanish all;
The City of God remaineth.

MARTIN LUTHER (1483–1546)
translated by THOMAS CARLYLE (1795–1881)

WHO WOULD
TRUE VALOUR SEE

Christiana and her four sons are nearing the goal of the pilgrimage when they meet a wounded man on the road. His name is Mr Valiant-for-Truth. They wash his wounds, give him food and drink, and learn his story as they travel on together.

Spurred on by the example of Christian himself, Mr Valiant-for-Truth had set out on the journey from the City of Destruction to the Celestial City. He relates the obstacles and battles along the way and, since pilgrims love to sing, launches into 'Who would true valour see . . .

This is just a part of John Bunyan's masterpiece, *The Pilgrim's Progress*, an allegory of a Christian's spiritual pilgrimage. Now a classic of English literature, it was written while Bunyan was imprisoned in Bedford jail. He was persecuted for his faith and his preaching — but though his voice was silenced for a while, his pen was not.

Who would true valour see,
  Let him come hither;
One here will constant be,
  Come wind, come weather.
There's no discouragement
Shall make him once relent
His first avowed intent
  To be a pilgrim.

Who so beset him round
  With dismal stories,
Do but themselves confound;
  His strength the more is.
No lion can him fright,
He'll with a giant fight,
But he will have a right
  To be a pilgrim.

Hobgoblin nor foul fiend
  Can daunt his spirit;
He knows he at the end
  Shall life inherit.
Then fancies fly away;
He'll fear not what men say;
He'll labour night and day
  To be a pilgrim.

JOHN BUNYAN (1628–88)

ABIDE WITH ME

At the FA Cup Final at Wembley Stadium in April 1927, Cardiff City's 1-0 victory over Arsenal took football's oldest trophy out of England for the first and only time.

That match was also another 'first'. King George V was one of the 100,000 crowd who sang 'Abide with me' at a Wembley final for the first time. And since 1927 the hymn has always had a special link with Wembley. These words are now heard every Cup Final afternoon by a television audience of over 15 million in Britain alone, and by many more millions on radio and television around the world.

Abide with me; fast falls the eventide;
The darkness deepens; Lord, with me abide!
When other helpers fail, and comforts flee,
Help of the helpless, O abide with me.

Swift to its close ebbs out life's little day;
Earth's joys grow dim, its glories pass away;
Change and decay in all around I see;
O thou who changest not, abide with me.

I need thy presence every passing hour;
What but thy grace can foil the tempter's power?
Who like thyself my guide and stay can be?
Through cloud and sunshine, O abide with me.

I fear no foe with thee at hand to bless;
Ills have no weight, and tears no bitterness.
Where is death's sting? where, grave, thy victory?
I triumph still, if thou abide with me.

Hold thou thy cross before my closing eyes;
Shine through the gloom, and point me to the skies;
Heaven's morning breaks, and earth's vain shadows flee;
In life, in death, O Lord, abide with me!

HENRY FRANCIS LYTE (1793-1847)

THROUGH ALL
THE CHANGING SCENES OF LIFE

'Tate and Brady' were once as familiar and inseparable a pair of names as Laurel and Hardy or Rodgers and Hammerstein.

They were Irish Protestants whose *New Version* of metrical psalms, published in 1696, replaced the so-called *Old Version* of the previous generation. This version of part of Psalm 34 is the one survivor that has stayed the course for nearly three centuries.

But new versions always have their critics. Brady's own church would have none of it; to them it was 'an innovation not to be endured'. And Tate's brother had a maid who refused to come to family prayers because of it. 'As long as you sang Jesus Christ's psalms, I sung along with ye,' she said. 'But now that you sing psalms of your own invention, ye may sing by yourselves!'

Through all the changing scenes of life,
  In trouble and in joy,
The praises of my God shall still
  My heart and tongue employ.

The hosts of God encamp around
  The dwellings of the just;
Deliverance he affords to all
  Who on his succour trust.

O magnify the Lord with me,
  With me exalt his name;
When in distress to him I called,
  He to my rescue came.

O make but trial of his love,
  Experience will decide
How blest they are, and only they,
  Who in his truth confide.

Fear him, ye saints, and you will then
  Have nothing else to fear;
Make you his service your delight,
  Your wants shall be his care.

NAHUM TATE (1652–1715)
NICHOLAS BRADY (1659–1726)

WHAT A FRIEND
WE HAVE IN JESUS

On the eve of Joseph Scriven's intended wedding-day, his bride-to-be was tragically drowned. Later he emigrated from Ireland to Canada. Once again he became engaged to be married, only to lose his second fiancée after a brief but fatal illness.

In spite of loneliness, poverty and his own precarious health, he spent the rest of his life helping the physically handicapped, as well as teaching and ministering among his fellow Christian Brethren in Ontario.

But it was not his own troubles that led him to write this hymn. He sent the words to his mother when she was going through a very distressing time. So, as with many other hymns, a private message has become a source of comfort to people across the world.

What a Friend we have in Jesus
All our sins and griefs to bear;
What a privilege to carry
Everything to God in prayer.
O what peace we often forfeit,
O what needless pain we bear;
All because we do not carry
Everything to God in prayer.

Have we trials and temptations?
Is there trouble anywhere?
We should never be discouraged;
Take it to the Lord in prayer.
Can we find a friend so faithful
Who will all our sorrows share?
Jesus knows our every weakness;
Take it to the Lord in prayer.

Are we weak and heavy-laden,
Cumbered with a load of care?
Precious Saviour, still our refuge —
Take it to the Lord in prayer.
Do thy friends despise, forsake thee?
Take it to the Lord in prayer;
In his arms he'll take and shield thee,
Thou wilt find a solace there.

JOSEPH MEDLICOTT SCRIVEN (1819–86)

ETERNAL FATHER,
STRONG TO SAVE

By 1950, the American writer Albert E.
Bailey had made the Atlantic crossing by sea forty-nine
times. And every Sunday on board, he says, this hymn
was sung at the ship's morning service.

It is sung in war and peace, on great
public occasions as well as by lifeboatmen or fishermen in
lonely coastal villages — and now in many languages
around the world too. It is only surprising that it was
written by a landsman — a short, bespectacled
schoolmaster whose health was never robust.

Eternal Father, strong to save,
Whose arm doth bind the restless wave,
Who bidd'st the mighty ocean deep
Its own appointed limits keep:
  O hear us when we cry to thee
  For those in peril on the sea.

O Christ, whose voice the waters heard
And hushed their raging at thy word,
Who walkedst on the foaming deep,
And calm amid the storm didst sleep:
  O hear us when we cry to thee
  For those in peril on the sea.

O Holy Spirit, who didst brood
Upon the waters dark and rude,
And bid their angry tumult cease,
And give, for wild confusion, peace:
  O hear us when we cry to thee
  For those in peril on the sea.

O Trinity of love and power,
Our brethren shield in danger's hour;
From rock and tempest, fire and foe,
Protect them wheresoe'er they go:
  Thus evermore shall rise to thee
  Glad hymns of praise from land and sea.

WILLIAM WHITING (1825-78)

JUST AS I AM

A white-haired, hard-hitting Southern Baptist preacher called Mordecai Ham was leading an eleven-week evangelistic campaign in the town of Charlotte, South Carolina, in September 1934.

Among his crowd of listeners was a local farmer's son — tall, good-looking William Franklin Graham. He had not been too keen to attend — religion to him was 'all hogwash' — but this evangelist held him spellbound. One night, as the choir sang 'Just as I am', the young man walked to the front, as a sign of his new-found faith in Christ, the Lamb of God.

Billy Graham has since become a world figure. He has spoken live to more people than any other man in history. And in every continent, in his own evangelistic crusades, he has used the hymn that meant so much to him.

Just as I am — without one plea.
But that thy blood was shed for me,
And that thou bidst me come to thee,
O Lamb of God, I come.

Just as I am — though tossed about
With many a conflict, many a doubt,
Fightings and fears within, without —
O Lamb of God, I come.

Just as I am — thou wilt receive,
Wilt welcome, pardon, cleanse, relieve,
Because thy promise I believe —
O Lamb of God, I come.

Just as I am — thy love unknown
Has broken every barrier down;
Now to be thine, yea, thine alone —
O Lamb of God, I come.

Just as I am — of that free love
The breadth, length, depth and height to prove,
Here for a season, then above —
O Lamb of God, I come.

CHARLOTTE ELLIOTT (1789-1871)

DEAR LORD
AND FATHER OF MANKIND

'I am really not a hymn writer', said the American poet who wrote these verses. And few who started to read *The Brewing of Soma* by John Greenleaf Whittier would guess what was coming. It is a long poem, describing at first how 'soma', an intoxicating drink, was made to prepare Indian worshippers for their frenzied Vedic rites. By way of contrast, at the end of the poem, Whittier turns to the God and Father of our Lord Jesus Christ.

Within twelve years of the poem's publication, these five verses were being used separately as a Christian hymn, and few now remember their origin. Whittier belonged to the Society of Friends, or Quakers, who, more than most Christian groups, have discovered the value of meditative silence in their worship of God.

Dear Lord and Father of mankind,
  Forgive our foolish ways!
Re-clothe us in our rightful mind,
In purer lives thy service find,
  In deeper reverence praise.

In simple trust like theirs who
    heard,
  Beside the Syrian sea,
The gracious calling of the Lord,
Let us, like them, without a word
  Rise up and follow thee.

O Sabbath rest by Galilee!
  O calm of hills above,
Where Jesus knelt to share with
    thee
The silence of eternity,
  Interpreted by love!

Drop thy still dews of quietness,
  Till all our strivings cease;
Take from our souls the strain and
    stress,
And let our ordered lives confess
  The beauty of thy peace.

Breathe through the heats of our
    desire
  Thy coolness and thy balm;
Let sense be dumb, let flesh retire;
Speak through the earthquake,
    wind, and fire,
  O still small voice of calm!

JOHN GREENLEAF WHITTIER (1807-92)

LEAD US,
HEAVENLY FATHER, LEAD US

If James Edmeston were to return to his native east London today — he was born at Wapping and 'died at Hackney — he would not easily recognize his surroundings. New housing estates and tower blocks have taken over where bombs fell or old buildings crumbled. It is even less likely that he would see many of the buildings which he, as an architect and surveyor, designed. However, the parish church of St Barnabas still stands in Homerton High Street. Edmeston was churchwarden there for many years.

This hymn, among 2,000 others he wrote, has outlived any of his environmental achievements and is now firmly established as a favourite choice at wedding services.

Lead us, heavenly Father, lead us
   O'er the world's tempestuous
      sea;
Guard us, guide us, keep us, feed
   us,
   For we have no help but thee;
Yet possessing every blessing
   If our God our Father be.

Saviour, breathe forgiveness o'er us,
   All our weakness thou dost
      know,
Thou didst tread this earth before us,
   Thou didst feel its keenest woe;
Son of Mary, lone and weary,
   Victor through this world
      didst go.

Spirit of our God, descending,
   Fill our hearts with heavenly joy,
Love with every passion blending,
   Pleasure that can never cloy:
Thus provided, pardoned, guided,
   Nothing can our peace destroy.

JAMES EDMESTON (1791–1867)

COME, HOLY GHOST, OUR SOULS INSPIRE

In 1649, the reign of King Charles I of England came to a sudden and violent end — on the scaffold. But twenty-four years earlier it had begun splendidly enough, at a coronation service full of colourful pageantry and ceremonial. And one of the churchmen officiating then was John Cosin, later Bishop of Durham, who had produced a hymn specially for the great occasion.

It was a translation of a Latin work already some eight centuries old. Long before hymns became a regular part of church services in English, Cosin's version won its way as one of the only two hymns in the 1662 *Book of Common Prayer*.

Come, Holy Ghost, our souls inspire,
And lighten with celestial fire;
Thou the anointing Spirit art,
Who dost thy sevenfold gifts impart:

Thy blessèd unction from above
Is comfort, life, and fire of love;
Enable with perpetual light
The dullness of our blinded sight:

Anoint and cheer our soilèd face
With the abundance of thy grace:
Keep far our foes, give peace at home;
Where thou art guide no ill can come.

Teach us to know the Father, Son,
And thee, of Both, to be but One;
That through the ages all along
This may be our endless song,
  Praise to thy eternal merit,
  Father, Son, and Holy Spirit. Amen.

JOHN COSIN (1594-1672)

O COME,
O COME, EMMANUEL

John Mason Neale was a born scholar.
Before he was ten, he edited his own handwritten family
magazine. As a shy but strong-minded young man, he could
often be seen making a brass-rubbing or collecting
architectural details in country churches he visited on his
walking-tours.

He grew up to love the Middle Ages and the medieval
church, the early church fathers and the lives of the saints.
One small girl at his orphanage said that Mr Neale (then in his
forties) 'must be very old, to have talked to so many saints
and martyrs'.

This Advent hymn is from a Latin original of doubtful
date. As the greatest of all translators of hymns, Neale helped
to disprove his friend Benjamin Webb's words: 'I am more
and more convinced that the age of hymns has passed'!

O come, O come, Emmanuel,
And ransom captive Israel.
That mourns in lonely exile here,
Until the Son of God appear.
Rejoice! Rejoice! Emmanuel
Shall come to thee, O Israel.

O come, thou Rod of Jesse, free
Thine own from Satan's tyranny;
From depths of hell thy people save,
And give them victory o'er the grave.

O come, thou Dayspring, come
and cheer
Our spirits by thine advent here;
Disperse the gloomy clouds of night,
And death's dark shadows put to
flight.

O come, thou Key of David, come,
And open wide our heavenly home;
Make safe the way that leads on
high,
And close the path to misery.

O come, O come, thou Lord of
Might,
Who to thy tribes, on Sinai's height,
In ancient times didst give the law
In cloud and majesty and awe.

From the Latin; translated by JOHN MASON NEALE (1818–66)

ONCE, IN ROYAL DAVID'S CITY

For millions of radio listeners all over the world, Christmas begins with the clear treble voice of a Cambridge choirboy. Every year since 1919, this has been the opening hymn in the Service of Nine Lessons and Carols broadcast from King's College Chapel on Christmas Eve.

The hymn itself is much older than this particular service. It is one of the 1848 collection by Mrs Alexander, written to illustrate the words from the Apostles' Creed: '. . . born of the virgin Mary'.

Once in royal David's city,
  Stood a lowly cattle-shed,
Where a mother laid her baby
  In a manger for his bed.
Mary was that mother mild,
Jesus Christ her little child.

He came down to earth from
      heaven,
  Who is God and Lord of all;
And his shelter was a stable
  And his cradle was a stall.
With the poor and mean and lowly
Lived on earth our Saviour holy.

And through all his wondrous
      childhood
  He would honour and obey,
Love, and watch the lowly maiden
  In whose gentle arms he lay.
Christian children all must be
Mild, obedient, good as he.

For he is our childhood's pattern;
  Day by day like us he grew.
He was little, weak, and helpless;
  Tears and smiles like us he knew:
And he feeleth for our sadness
And he shareth in our gladness.

Not in that poor lowly stable
  With the oxen standing by
We shall see him, but in heaven,
  Set at God's right hand on high,
When like stars his children
      crowned
All in white shall wait around.

And our eyes at last shall see him,
  Through his own redeeming love;
For that child so dear and gentle
  Is our Lord in heaven above:
And he leads his children on
To the place where he is gone.

CECIL FRANCES ALEXANDER (1818-95)

O COME,
ALL YE FAITHFUL

Young William Ewart Gladstone, who later became British Prime Minister, greatly appreciated the services at Margaret Chapel in London's West End. For one thing, the sermons were short — never more than twenty minutes! More important, the congregation were 'the most devout and hearty that I have ever seen'.

The minister at that time was Frederick Oakeley — one of the leaders of the nineteenth-century Oxford Movement. He believed passionately in the power of ritual, religious symbols and fine music. And before he joined the Roman Catholic Church, he gave his congregation — and the world — this version of the eighteenth-century 'Adeste, fideles'.

O come, all ye faithful,
Joyful and triumphant,
O come ye, O come ye to Bethlehem;
Come and behold him,
Born the King of angels:
O come, let us adore him,
O come, let us adore him,
O come, let us adore him, Christ the Lord.

God of God,
Light of Light,
Lo! he abhors not the virgin's
    womb;
Very God,
Begotten not created:

Sing, choirs of angels,
Sing, in exultation,
Sing, all ye citizens of heaven
    above,
'Glory to God
In the highest':

Yea, Lord, we greet thee,
Born this happy morning,
Jesu, to thee be glory given!
Word of the Father,
Now in flesh appearing:

FREDERICK OAKELEY (1802-80)

JOY TO THE WORLD!
THE LORD IS COME!

As the world's leading gospel singer prior to her death in 1972, Mahalia Jackson mixed with princesses and presidents, film-stars and top entertainers. But she turned down countless lucrative offers from bars, night-clubs and theatres — anywhere that liquor was sold. And she never sang the blues. considering it 'Devil's music'.

As a child in the poverty of New Orleans, Mahalia started singing. 'Hand me down my silver trumpet, Gabriel' was a life-long favourite, but so were the 'old Dr Watts' hymns of her Baptist church.

One Christmas, a blizzard stopped her going from Chicago to Memphis, where she was due to sing for civil rights workers in the negro college. So she called the telephone company, and from 8358 Indiana she held the 'phone for half an hour, and sang: 'Born in Bethlehem', 'Silent Night' and the 'old Dr Watts' — 'Joy to the World!'

Joy to the world! the Lord is come!
  Let earth receive her King!
Let every heart prepare him room,
  And heaven and nature sing.

Joy to the earth! the Saviour reigns!
  Let men their songs employ!
While fields and floods, rocks,
    hills, and plains
  Repeat the sounding joy.

No more let sins and sorrows grow,
  Nor thorns infest the ground;
He comes to make his blessings flow
  Far as the curse is found.

He rules the world with truth and
    grace,
  And makes the nations prove
The glories of his righteousness,
  And wonders of his love.

ISAAC WATTS (1674–1748)

HARK!
THE HERALD-ANGELS SING

On Christmas Day 1738, Charles Wesley preached at St Mary's Church in Islington, and gave the wine at Holy Communion. Next day it was George Whitefield's turn. 'We had the sacrament this and the four following days — the whole week was a festival indeed; a joyful season, holy unto the Lord.'

Was that the first Christmas ever to be enriched by this hymn? In its original version, it was published a few months later; Whitefield was one of those who afterwards shaped it to its present form.

So whenever we sing these words today, we are heirs to the work of England's finest hymn-writer and her greatest preacher.

The composer Mendelssohn belongs to the next century, but he did not live long enough to hear his famous music matched with this magnificent hymn.

Hark! the herald-angels sing
Glory to the new-born King,
Peace on earth, and mercy mild,
God and sinners reconciled.
Joyful, all ye nations, rise,
Join the triumph of the skies;
With the angelic host proclaim
'Christ is born in Bethlehem.
Hark! the herald-angels sing
Glory to the new-born King.

Christ, by highest heaven adored,
Christ, the everlasting Lord,
Late in time behold him come,
Offspring of a virgin's womb.
Veiled in flesh the Godhead see!
Hail, the incarnate Deity!
Pleased as Man with man to dwell,
Jesus, our Emmanuel.

Hail, the heaven-born Prince of Peace!
Hail, the Sun of Righteousness!
Light and life to all he brings,
Risen with healing in his wings.
Mild he lays his glory by,
Born that man no more may die,
Born to raise the sons of earth,
Born to give them second birth.

CHARLES WESLEY (1707–88) and others

GLORY TO THEE, MY GOD, THIS NIGHT

Thomas Ken wrote these words for the boys of Winchester College. A pastor at heart, he disliked controversy. But he felt he had to cross swords with three successive kings of England on matters of principle.

While at Winchester, he refused to put his house at the disposal of Nell Gwyn, mistress of Charles II, during a royal visit. But Charles bore no malice; when the bishopric of Bath and Wells fell vacant, he said, 'Where is the little fellow who refused poor Nelly a lodging? Give it to him!'

Ken remained a loyal bishop under James II; but he resisted the monarch's increasingly illegal measures, to the point of being imprisoned in the Tower of London. And when William and Mary came to the throne, he would not take the Oath of Allegiance. Because he considered that his oath to the exiled James still held good, he was deprived of his position in the church and in public life.

> Glory to thee, my God, this night
> For all the blessings of the light;
> Keep me, O keep me, King of kings,
> Under thy own almighty wings.

Forgive me, Lord, for thy dear Son,
The ill that I this day have done,
That with the world, myself, and
   thee,
I, e'er I sleep, at peace may be.

Teach me to live, that I may dread
The grave as little as my bed;
Teach me to die, that so I may
Triumphing rise at the last day.

O may my soul on thee repose,
And with sweet sleep mine eyelids
   close —
Sleep that may me more vigorous
   make
To serve my God when I awake.

When in the night I sleepless lie,
My soul with heavenly thoughts
   supply;
Let no ill dreams disturb my rest,
No powers of darkness me molest.

> Praise God from whom all blessings flow,
> Praise him, all creatures here below;
> Praise him above, ye heavenly host,
> Praise Father, Son, and Holy Ghost.

THOMAS KEN (1637–1711)

THE DAY THOU GAVEST

By 1897 Queen Victoria had been Britain's sovereign for sixty years; no other English monarch had reigned so long. The Diamond Jubilee was celebrated in tens of thousands of churches — and centrally in London at Westminster Abbey. This hymn was specially chosen by the queen to be sung in every church on that occasion.

In the hymn-books it is usually found in the 'Evening' section; but John Ellerton wrote it, while a vicar in Crewe, for missionary meetings. Christians in the nineteenth century were becoming aware of their responsibility to take the gospel to the whole world, and this hymn clearly expresses their international vision. Even when Victoria's empire had crumbled away, the kingdom of Christ would remain.

The day thou gavest, Lord, is ended,
    The darkness falls at thy behest;
To thee our morning hymns ascended,
    Thy praise shall sanctify our rest.

We thank thee that thy Church unsleeping,
    While earth rolls onward into light,
Through all the world her watch is keeping,
    And rests not now by day or night.

As o'er each continent and island
    The dawn leads on another day,
The voice of prayer is never silent,
    Nor dies the strain of praise away.

The sun that bids us rest is waking
    Our brethren 'neath the western sky,
And hour by hour fresh lips are making
    Thy wondrous doings heard on high.

So be it, Lord; thy throne shall never,
    Like earth's proud empires, pass away;
Thy Kingdom stands, and grows for ever,
    Till all thy creatures own thy sway.

JOHN ELLERTON (1826-93)